AF316804

Sometimes, life takes us on journeys we didn't ask for. But remember, no matter where you are, you are strong, brave, and full of dreams. This is just one part of your story, not the whole of who you are.

My name is Shams. I am from Sudan.
My name means the Sun.
I used to love playing under the sun in
front of our home. Running and
laughing with my friends.

Home was warm and full of love,
with my family and friends always
close.

I learned new things every day,

dreaming big dreams

in my safe school.

One day, everything changed.

The skies filled with danger.

We had to leave our home and

go far, far away.

We found safety in a
a refugee camp.

After walking for hours.

It was safe, but it was not home.

Even here,
I found new friends, and we laugh and
play when we can.

But,

I miss my soft bed, my cozy pillow, a
warm shower and the smells from Mom's
kitchen.

We eat, and sometimes we are not full,

but I try to help my family, and we try to

make the best of every day.

I, just like you, want to
live in a safe place.

I want a safe place to
call home again.

Bad things happened,

but we still believe in a better,

safer tomorrow for us and for

everyone around the world.